tweet her and meet her

The Man's Manual to Get Her Off Twitter

Written by Flyness™

**THE ULTIMATE REFERENCE GUIDE
FOR MEETING WOMEN VIA TWITTER!**

thanks

Thanks to The Princess, Phil, Leon, Angela, my fellow macks, and everyone who's supported all of my books to date! But this one is a classic!

As with each of my books, there was a lot of time and effort that went into putting this book together. The process took many hours over the course of many months. That means that this information has value and your friends, neighbors, and co-workers may want to share it. The price of this book is very small, compared to the value you are getting from it. So, if your friends like the concept of the book, please encourage them to purchase their own copy from **www.TweetHerAndMeetHer.com.**

Make sure you follow @Flyness on Twitter and check out his other titles at www.FlynessPublishing.com!

Tweet Her And Meet Her, by Flyness™
Flyness Publishing, a division of Flyness Media LLC

ISBN: 978-0-578-07972-1

All contents copyright © 2011 Flyness Publishing, a division of Flyness Media LLC

No part of this document may be reproduced or transmitted in any form, by any means (electronic, photocopying, recording, or otherwise) without the prior written permission of the publisher. All rights reserved.
Twitter is a trademark of Twitter, Inc. We are not associated with Twitter, or Twitter.com in any way, shape, or form.

table of contents

chapter one – your profile 10

chapter two – finding your "twargets" 20

chapter three – the breakdown 27

chapter four – contacting her for the first time 50

chapter five – sealing the deal and taking it offline 58

chapter six – major twitfalls 71

chapter seven – "speed tweeting" 79

chapter eight – getting at twitter celebrities 93

chapter nine – organizing your "twitchicks" 99

chapter ten – bonus tips 105

glossary of online abbreviations and emoticons 112

recommended reads 115

book flyness 117

introduction

Writing this book will be extremely therapeutic for me. Why? This is because Twitter has allowed me to return to my roots of raw "online game". Those of you who have utilized AOL Instant Messaging and AOL profiles before social networking sites took over know *exactly* what I'm talking about. Back then, there was usually only a single photo, and just a couple of clues about who the female was. To the novice "online dater", having so little information nowadays is unimaginable.

Although Twitter is among one of the newest social networking sites, the concept is far simpler than that of MySpace, Facebook and the slew of other sites. Instead of an HTML-enabled and customizable profile, and the ability to store hundreds of photos and detailed profile information, Twitter has imposed strict limits on its users. Instead of a nearly endless limit on messages, all tweets are limited to 140 characters. And while your profile background can be customized to whatever image you desire, you are limited to one main profile pic at a time, and have only a small amount of space to write vital information about yourself.

Why Twitter?

If you've read any of my previous titles, you'd know that I'm incredibly impatient. I love getting results and getting them *quickly*. I absolutely cannot stand waiting around for a reply or an answer. While some may attribute that to a negative trait, I actually think this is positive! Why? Allow me to digress for a moment.

The world, especially the western world is becoming increasingly rich in information sharing. There are a variety of ways we communicate now, which simply did not exist only twenty years ago: text messaging, emailing, instant messaging, and now "tweeting" to name a few. The fact is, people want answers and they want them *now*. Twitter is addressing this call, specifically by asking, "What are you doing" or "What's happening?" The "need to know now" is why Twitter has been so successful.

The dating world is no different. In the western world, especially in the United States, online dating has become incredibly popular. According to various web publications, including MSNBC.com, roughly 40 million American singles use online dating and social networking sites to meet new people. This figure makes up about 40% of single persons in the U.S.[1]

Having met hundreds of women online, I can attest to the ease and speed of meeting women in a short period of time. In two of my previous books, *From MySpace to My Place: The Men's Guide to Snagging Women Online* and *The Facebook Datebook for Men*, I included a chapter on how to bring a woman from an online encounter to the flesh within the hour. Where else is it possible to meet a woman and date her in the same day?

This Book

This book is every guy's all out reference guide to getting women on Twitter. Whether you aim to meet your future wife or just want to meet more quality women, this is *the* book for you. I have not only talked the talk, but I've walked the walk. Take a seat, grab a highlighter, and read on "playas"!

---

[1] Author: Unknown. "Current Online Dating and Dating Services Facts & Statistics." Datingsitesreviews.com. Last Updated: Friday, December 24 2010

disclaimers and faq's

Are you teaching men how to "play" women and take advantage of them?

Yes! I'm kidding. Of course not. I find it ironic that even after publishing three books, I still get these questions. This book teaches men how to "upgrade" their game—not by deception, but by projecting confidence, using strategy, and becoming more straightforward with women.

What qualifies you to write this book?

This is one of the most common questions I have been asked about all of my books. As an early teen, I had no game. In many ways, I was the stereotypical geek—good grades, but no girls. I longed for women who had no interest in me, and thought by being the proverbial "Mr. Nice Guy," I would eventually attract women. As an introvert who moved around a lot, I practiced my game via phone chat-lines and eventually the internet chatrooms and AOL Instant Messanger. I began to get good. As time grew on, I sought game from those who were successful with women, read a lot of books, and began to apply those principles to my own life—specifically in the online dating world.

Over the past 12 years or so, I've met hundreds of women from all over the internet, some of which have been celebrities, models and notable people. Before going on vacations, I've used sites like Facebook, MySpace and Twitter to meet girls at my destination. For the fun of it, I've actually lined up hundreds of females to meet me at some of my favorite vacation spots. I've also brought women to an in-person meeting within hours and *even minutes* of first contacting them online.

Around five years ago, my friends and associates recommended I put together a manual on the subject. I resisted at first, but finally gave in. I'm glad I did. Since December 2007, I've now written four books helping both men and women traverse the world of online dating via social networking sites. Simply put, I wrote these books because I've done it. I've mastered it. And I've helped others to do the same.

Why another book for Online Dating?

Twitter is a site that involves a different kind of strategy from MySpace and Facebook. Although the general principles of self-confidence and boldness still hold true, the correct ways to meet women must be done strategically. For instance, as opposed to MySpace and Facebook, careful attention must be paid to the number of followers your interest has. As I will explain further in Chapter 3, a wrong move with a celebrity or blogger may permanently damage your Twitter reputation. While Twitter is really only a site of "updates", you must be strategic in your approach.

What do you mean by the terms, *player* and *game*?

When many people hear these words, they immediately conjure up images of lies, deceit and deception. A *player* in the mind of most people is someone who intentionally deceives women for sex, money and other items of personal gain. In the mind of most people, *game* is the way in which he achieves these lies. This **is not** what a "true player" or possessing "true game" is.

Let's break down the definition of *Game* and *Player*.

Game

The dictionary defines "game" as,

> ...a competitive activity involving skill, chance, or endurance on the part of two or more persons who play according to a set of rules, usually for their own amusement or for that of spectators.[2]

As my mentor and associate Tariq "King Flex" Nasheed has said on many occasions, life in itself is a game since we must abide by a set of rules and guidelines to achieve certain objectives. We have laws, rules, and behaviors in which we follow to achieve a given result. Dating is no different. Possessing game is vital as it is the only way you will achieve success in the dating world.

Player

Let go of the stereotypical image of a man sneaking into and out of the homes of his "baby mommas". A player is not the man on Maury Povich who impregnated the entire panel. He is actually the "anti-player". A real player is honest with his woman or women. He doesn't hide the fact that he is dating or "kickin it with other ladies". He doesn't have to lie about his possessions or image to attract women. On the contrary, it is because of his attitude and "swagger" that he is able to garner and keep women. Simply put, a *player* is a person who possesses *game*.

How do I book you for an event, function or speaking engagement?

Easy. You can contact me directly at flynesspublishing@gmail.com or simply go to http://www.GetHerOnTwitter.com.

---

[2] "game." The American Heritage® Dictionary of Idioms by Christine Ammer. Houghton Mifflin Company. 04 Jan. 2010. <Dictionary.com http://dictionary.reference.com/browse/game>.

twitter 101

Before I discuss "the game" on Twitter, you should already be familiar with the website. For those of you who are *newbies*, here is a crash course. Twitter is a free social networking and "micro-blogging" site that allows its users to send and read messages. These messages are known as **tweets**. Each tweet is limited to 140 characters and is displayed on the author's page, along with the pages of the author's subscribers, otherwise known as ***followers***.

You may follow or unfollow someone at your heart's content. If you wish to tweet someone (also known as a **reply**), you can simply type the "@" symbol before their screen name followed by a character space and continue with your message. For example, to say "Hi" to **Flyness** on Twitter, simply type, **@Flyness Hi**.

If you like someone else's Tweet, you may elect to "retweet" it by clicking the "retweet" button below a message or by typing "RT" followed by a character space before a reply. For example, if Flyness tweeted, "Get some game!" and you find this information useful, you may retweet this message by tweeting, **RT @Flyness Get some game!**

It is strongly suggested that you familiarize yourself with Twitter before becoming a "TwitterMack". The game in this book is powerful and can do some damage if it fell into the hands of a novice!

chapter one – your profile

In just about every conversation I've had with people who've never purchased my books, the first thing everyone wants to know is what pickup line to use in order to get a woman's attention online. This is the mentality that causes most men to fail. In each of my books, I've stressed the importance of establishing "who you are" before "what you say." The "who you are" on any social networking site is your profile.

Fellas, make sure *your profile* on Twitter is attractive and "crispy". Focusing on getting a woman's attention solely through a clever message or "tweet" and ignoring important aspects of your profile is like someone selling an attractive appliance that doesn't work. You may turn a few heads, but your customers would be unhappy. Your game would be shallow and transparent. As opposed to the increasing number of books geared to online dating (and dating in general), I do not teach gimmicks and "gags". The game enclosed in this book is real and tested by me. And I can verify every sentence in this book. Let's get into the game!

YOUR DISPLAY NAME / URL

Everyone on Twitter has their own display name. You may be as creative as you wish, but keep in mind that this is your identity. You can change your display name at any time, yet I do not recommend doing it often. Changing your display name can make you more difficult to find and may slow down the speed at which you gain more followers. This is especially true if you've already established yourself under a particular name. And as we will discuss later in the chapter, having more followers will greatly improve your prospects with eMackin'.

Five Things to Avoid when Choosing a Display Name

1. Anything sexually suggestive
2. Violent Themes or Imagery
3. Anything that puts your sexuality into question
4. Buffoonery
5. "Simpery"

Sexually Suggestive Display Names

Time and time again, guys make the fatal mistake of acting too perverted with women. Nothing turns a woman off quicker than a pervert. Choosing display names like "InYourThighs" or "SuckYourNips" or "8inch4U" is generally not a good idea. While you might garner a few laughs, you are working against yourself. Even if a woman you are targeting is a freak, associating herself with you may give her the appearance of appearing *too* slutty. And no woman wants to be known as a slut. Unless you are an experienced player, I suggest staying away from names that hint at sexual themes.

Violent Themes or Imagery

Another trap a lot of guys fall into is picking violent display names—especially young guys. First off, if you have a Twitter account, you're not a "gangsta", nor a thug. Display names like "21Guns2shoot" or "murderUnow" make you sound fake. Moreover, you sound as though you're overcompensating for something. Most women will be immediately turned off by a violent display name. Don't do it!

Display Names putting sexual orientation into question

Let me start off by saying there is nothing wrong with being gay, whatsoever. How you choose to live your life is not up to me to judge. However if you are *not* gay, please be mindful of your display name. Names like "barebttom" or "hunglong" are both sexually suggestive and hint at homosexuality. On the flipside, names that spell out your affinity for designer clothing at women's stores like "loveprada" may call your sexuality into question as well. Fellas, this book is called, **Tweet Her And**

Meet Her. If that is your goal, avoid the questionable display names!

Buffoonery

Incorporating humor is a good thing and can be very effective if done correctly. However, there's a difference between being *comedic* and being a *buffoon*. An example of buffoonery is when someone goes completely overboard to get attention. For example, I've seen display names which poke fun at celebrities' body parts. An example would be @LadyGagasLeftTitty. It will get a chuckle, but what female would take you seriously? How do you even take yourself serious with a display name like this? Being humorous is encouraged, but save the buffoonery.

Simpery

"Simpery" is the act of being a "simp", or an extreme kiss-ass and brown-noser. Your most common "simps" are guys who agree with everything a woman says in order not to "stir the pot". An example of "simpin" in your profile would be choosing a display name like @iLuvWomen or @WillYouBeMyQueen. Attempts made to overtly (or even covertly) brown-nose are transparent. Women are used to being pandered to and rarely find this attractive. Be a man's man and stay away from "simpish" behavior.

YOUR PROFILE PIC

I cannot stress the importance of a good twitter profile photo. Unlike MySpace, Facebook, PlentyofFish and the rest, Twitter allows one pic in your profile.[3] That means you have to make it count! Whatever you decide to wear in the pic, make sure it's clear and keep it interesting. Give people something entertaining to look at. Moreover, give the LADIES something to look at.

With that said, stay away from pictures with your shirt off and showing the "V" near your pubic region. If you really want to know how women feel about men with their shirts off in their social networking sites, visit http://www.youtube.com/FlynessPublishing and go to the video titled, "From MySpace To My Place Model Interview". In that video, I interview one of my promotional models who expressed her disgust at guys who go overboard online. As she puts it, it makes you seem as if you have no life and that you're "not getting any ass" at home.

---

[3] As of May 2010

TWITPICS AND *TWITVIDS*

Twitter has many spin-off applications which allow users to post links to photos and videos in their timelines. Similar to your profile pics, make sure these photos and videos show you in a positive light. Always be mindful of your image…even in a relaxed setting, always present yourself as the type of guy who is worthy of the *best* women. Whether you're on vacation, at a wedding, or just around the house, come across as a boss.

YOUR PROFILE BIO

Twitter allows its users only 160 characters for a biography. This in itself is saving a lot of guys from looking like blabbermouths. On other social networking sites such as Facebook, it's easy for guys to get carried away. Thankfully, Twitter profiles do not give you a choice. For this area, be imaginative. In fact, feel free to experiment with your bio and see how it works for you. Whatever the case, make sure you accomplish two things: 1) capture at least a piece of "who you are" and 2) add some spice.

Capturing who you are is simple: just be *you*. If you're kind of a geek, be a cool geek. Whatever the case, just don't go overboard. As I will talk about later, women can tell when you're trying *too* hard. Never appear needy as this will single-handedly kill your game. All in all, there is no "right" thing to say. Find your angle and use it!

GETTING MORE FOLLOWERS

Are you trying to win a popularity contest or are you trying to meet cute women on Twitter? Fellas, do not get too caught up in gaining followers. I'll admit, having more followers gives you "TwitterStar Power". However, becoming overly obsessed with your following will have you doing unnatural things, just because you'll be trying to please your "tweeps." The best way to gain more followers is to be interesting. Be witty. Invoke replies (when people tweet you a message), and retweets (when people quote you). Participate in "TT"s" or "Trending Topics" every now and then. But again fellas, don't go overboard. Do not be a male "attention whore".

MISCELLANOUS

Colors and Themes

I do not care how comfortable you are in your masculinity (or not), do *not* use pink, fuchsia or anything of the sort on your profile design page. Bright, feminine-leaning designs and colors in your profile may call into question your sexuality with some women. The worst thing about it is, you may never realize that this could be the reason why so many women are not messaging or following you.

Email Address and Web URL

In your profile, it is required that you enter a web URL and email address. These addresses and URLs are no exception to the rules above. Do not make them too sexually suggestive, violent, overly buffoon, or homosexual-leaning. And if you happen to have a website or email address in one of these categories, choose a different link and email. Email addresses are free and easy to create and a web URL can be your Facebook profile.

CONCLUSION

Fellas, all you really need to keep in mind is that you want to go against the grain of what most of these guys act like on Twitter.

Just as in real life, most men do the *wrong* things in their attempt to meet women to date. **You** are different. Always maintain your pride and dignity. Your profile speaks volumes. Let it say something to the women who happen to find you intriguing.

chapter two – finding your "twargets"

Unlike other social networking sites which normally include a "browse" feature, Twitter users need to utilize the "Find People" option. This gives you the option of discovering "Tweople" you have emailed before via Yahoo, Gmail, etc. However, this doesn't help you find *new* women. The "Find People" feature also lists popular categories so you can browse users. However, the categories are very general and do not currently include any filters for location, when they last logged in, or even gender. You can also search for their name or display name. That's a shot in the dark.

For these reasons, Twitter makes finding women you don't already know a tremendous challenge. However, they call me *Flyness* for a reason. Sit back and observe.

WAYS TO DISCOVER NEW WOMEN ON TWITTER
1. Other sites
2. Trending Topics
3. Mutual Friends
4. Hashtags based on location
5. New followers of your own

Other sites

Other social networking sites and Twitter actually compliment each other very nicely. Think of your "online macking" game like a wedding. If MySpace is the groom and Facebook is the bride, then Twitter is the Reverend. Think of Twitter as the way to link your online presence together.

Recently, MySpace users have been flocking to Facebook and Twitter to fulfill their social networking needs. This is in part due to the maturing of the "MySpace" generation. A New York Times article sums this up perfectly:

> "While Facebook is adding users, MySpace is losing them. Many user profile pages on MySpace are either cluttered or neglected, resembling a strip mall with pockets of empty storefronts. The users who remain tend to be younger and poorer, putting a drag on advertising revenue from blue-chip clients."[4]

In turn, many MySpace users now use their profiles to publicly advertise their Twitter accounts. It is not uncommon for MySpace users to update their status or change their display

---

[4] Stelter, Brian and Tim Arango. "Losing Popularity Contest, MySpace Tries a Makeover." New York Times. 5/3/2009, New York Edition: B3

names to "Follow me", and include their Twitter URLs. Believe it or not fellas, this is a great way to meet women. MySpace? Yes! Find her on MySpace, but "Tweet Her And Meet Her." The key is to use the "intel" from her MySpace profile so that your Twitter approach is smooth.

Trending Topics

This is another great way to "mix it up" and schmooze with potential prospects. Trending Topics (otherwise known as "TT's") are the ten most popular keywords or subjects on Twitter at any given moment. On the web-version of Twitter, the "TT's" are listed to the far right. Trending Topics vary and have included everything from comedic antidotes to shocking news of someone's passing. When clicking on a "TT", it is obviously preferred to stick to the more light-hearted topics. Once you click a topic, the most recent Tweet will be displayed at the top. Simply find a cute woman and make a response provoking message. Again, more on provoking a response in Chapter 4.

Mutual Friends

Periodically, platonic female friends of mine have spoken to (or **mentioned**) an attractive female twitter user. This is a great way to meet "female tweeps". On the internet, as well as in person, one of the most trusted ways to meet someone new is through a friend. This can be done either formally (the platonic friend introducing you two by mentioning both of you in a tweet), or simply by you introducing yourself to her. Let's say your platonic female friend has the twitter name, "brianaplatonic". If your friend mentions a cute woman, you can say something like, "I see you know my friend @brianaplatonic." You can follow this tweet with a compliment, such as on her photo (keeping it non-sexual) or her profile. If she is especially attractive, you can give her an ambiguous compliment such as, "…I'm glad @brianaplatonic's friends aren't hideous ;)" Be sure to include a wink or a smiley face to make sure you come across as humorous and avoid being perceived as a jerk!

Hashtags based on location

A hashtag on Twitter is simply a keyword, preceded by a "#" symbol. This word or phrase (which must not include any spaces), can be searched on. A good idea is to use this feature to search on larger neighborhoods in your vicinity.

One of my best friends uses this method in business. As a real estate agent, he's constantly "hashtaging" neighborhoods around him to see what is going on in an area and to contact people with an interest in that area. In most instances, these people currently live in or are planning to travel to that area. For instance, he might search #brooklyn, or even more specifically #bedstuy (a neighborhood in Brooklyn).

This technique can also be used for finding female prospects on Twitter. Test it out. In the search field, simply run a search against local cities, towns and neighborhoods and check out who's saying what. You're bound to find some cute women. Yeah, I know it is not a robust as MySpace or Facebook, which allow you to narrow down your prospects, by city and state; however, if done correctly, this is an effective way to meet new women.

New Followers

As your "buzz" grows on Twitter, so will your following. And if you followed the rules given in Chapter 1, women will notice and will begin to follow you, rather quickly. Make it a habit to stay *interesting* to prevent tweeps from unfollowing you. Every now and again, engage your female following by asking them how they are—even platonic friends. Other women will notice your dialogue and it will go a long way! Remember fellas, if a cute lady begins to follow you on Twitter, you already have her attention. So there's only one rule for this: don't screw it up!

In addition to these methods of finding female prospects on Twitter, it is very likely you will discover new tweeps from other users' timelines and other websites. Whatever the case, your goal is to be engaging and interesting. Do your best not to put your following to sleep!

And now, the breakdown…Twitter style!

chapter three – the breakdown

Now that you've found some ladies based on the tips given in Chapter 2, it's time to figure out what kind of woman she is. This will ultimately determine *how* you should deal with her. Knowing any woman's type, whether online or in real life, will tell you all you need to know on how to proceed. But don't worry fellas, I got you! Continue.

In each of my previous books, I dedicated an entire chapter on how to decipher between prospects you should approach, the ones to exercise caution with, and the ones to avoid. This chapter will be no different. However the brevity in Twitter's features presents unique challenges.

Unlike MySpace and especially Facebook profiles, which often contain long biographies along with dozens, if not hundreds of photos, Twitter yields very little info—at least on the surface. The lack of photos and "intel" in a user's profile makes breaking down potential ladies a little more challenging. The key to filling in the loose pieces of information is: her timeline.

Twitter gives its users a chance to vent. It is not uncommon for people to talk about very personal subjects such as break ups, sickness, and sadness online. Use her timeline to your advantage when "gathering intel" on a potential interest. Got it? Good.

There are *three main ways* you should view women on Twitter. The categories which will help you remember are as follows:

<u>Twitches</u> – The women you must avoid **at all costs**.

<u>Twobablies (sounds like "Probablies")</u> – The women you **may** "probably" choose to proceed with, but must do so with caution.

<u>Tweethearts</u> – The women you **should** go for.

TWITCHES

Twitter Thuggets and TwitTrash

Without exception, this is the worst type of female. Twitter thuggets and twit "trash" are the types of women who will not only bring the drama, but may also bring the bullets! If you're not ready to die, stay clear of this woman. Okay, while I might be exaggerating a bit, women from "the gutter" tend to have dealings with other "gutter" dudes. If you habitually deal with this type of female, you may have a run in with her ex. As opposed to "homegirls" who happen to live in "the hood" or "the park", thuggets are the ones who embrace the lifestyle. They are usually the ones who bad mouth people who attempt to get their education and do better for themselves. The point in all my books is for you guys to associate yourselves with *upstanding* women—even if it is just for a booty call. Attempting to "pop" some booty is *not* worth getting "popped" in yours!

Even though a twitter profile is short on photos, these types of women make it blatantly obvious who they are. In addition to an array of tattoos she might be showing off in her pic, watch for tweets which promote violence, drugs, or run down a consistent list of "R.I.P.'s". In any event, don't be her next victim!

Co-workers

Unless it is a job that you can afford to lose, do not attempt to date co-workers you meet on Twitter (or anywhere else). If your relationship fails, imagine what this does for you at work. Not to mention the rough economy, it is simply not wise to put a good job on the line. Seeing this person day in and day out may cause arguments and awkwardness. Who wants to be around that? As I have advised in my other books, ask to be introduced to her friends. In fact, it is cool to "follow" her Twitter account and introduce yourself that way. I will talk about how to talk to her Twitter friends in Chapter 4.

Obsessive Women

If you read any of my previous books, you'd know that there was once a woman I met off the internet who was the true definition of "obsessive". She would call at all hours of the night and even threatened to kill herself if we couldn't meet when she wanted. While it might seem cute or even flattering for a woman to chase after you, an obsessed woman will eventually drive you insane. Obsessive women also include jealous women who always suspect you of cheating. Obsessed women are also the ones who fall in love (or in lust) *too* quickly. As in my situation, I once had a woman who told me she loved me within days of meeting her. These are also the women who will go out of their way to "mark their territory"—that territory being *you*!

The way to tell if you're looking at the profile of an obsessive woman can be tricky. One tell-tale sign is if she is always tweeting about her shortcomings, especially when it has to do with relationships. When looking through her timeline, if the majority of her tweets have been about how she hates the single life, and how no one loves her, you are likely looking at the timeline of an obsessed woman. Also, watch out for women who give you *too much* attention. Is she *always* saying "hi" or checking on you? Is she smothering you? Watch out!

Have you ever seen the movie "Fatal Attraction"? This is one of my favorite movies—mostly because of how *real* it is. The main character in that movie was doomed the moment he slept with an obsessed woman. Fellas, do not let this be you!

Married Women

Twitter, like most of the internet, is a safe haven for unfulfilled married people. During my recent appearance on Dr. Phil, he stated that Facebook was cited in one out of five divorces. It would not surprise me if Twitter rivaled that, especially as it continues to grow in popularity. In any unfulfilled situation, our natural human instinct is to search for an escape. The internet is an easy escape as many of your online activities can easily go unnoticed by an unsuspecting spouse.

In spite of popular belief, women cheat just as much, if not *more* than men in many cases. Author, Susan Shapiro Barash has written several books discussing female infidelity. Among her findings, she believes that upwards of 60% of all woman will have an extramarital affair at some point.[5]

---

[5] Morales, Tatiana. "When Women Cheat." CBS News. 1/18/2005,
http://www.cbsnews.com/stories/2005/01/17/earlyshow/living/main667380.shtml

Due to the accessibility of new men online, many married women are on the prowl. So why stay away? Similar to the "thuggette", married women will undoubtedly have a husband out there who could potentially do you harm. It's one thing to fool around with a woman who has a boyfriend (that's bad enough). However, once you carry on a relationship with a married woman, you're playing with serious fire.

To tell if you're looking at the profile of a married woman, just look for the obvious. Does her profile pic show a ring on her ring finger? Is she hugged up with some guy in her photo? I admit, it is very easy to lie about your relationship status online. Yet do your due diligence during your "investigation" and always be on the lookout for **liars**! (next section)

Liars

This goes without saying. Lying women come in two categories: 1) women who will lie about anything, out of sheer habit, and 2) women who are lying to cover something up. In either case, run away! If a woman will lie *to* you, she will lie *about* you. I've heard of instances where disgruntled women will accuse men of rape or physical abuse out of spite. The worst part about liars is that even *she* may start to believe in her own lies. Be careful fellas.

To tell a liar on Twitter, be on the look out for women who consistently tell crazy tales. Like the time she dated R&B singer, "Trey Songz", or when Tom Cruise told her he loved her. Never give these women the time of day.

Broke Women

Beware, fellas. Due to the economy and the plethora of guys who are willing to exchange currency for booty, women are becoming increasingly bold in their pursuit for men with money. I'm not necessarily talking about men with riches either.

Having met so many women online, I have been noticing a steady, upward trend in broke women. Now more than ever, it seems that women expect to be wined and dined on the first date. Many times you won't be able to tell whether she's broke simply based on her profile or her tweets. However, after engaging her in a message exchange (which we will get to later), you will be able to tell rather quickly if she sees you as a meal ticket. If the emphasis is placed more on where you will be eating over getting to know you, she's literally starving. Stay clear, fellas!

Disrespectful Women

Nip this one in the bud, fellas. Disrespectful women are not even worth a one-nighter, in my opinion. Always have enough pride to demand and expect respect from any woman you deal with. Pride and manhood go hand in hand, so never allow anyone to take your pride away.

In society, more and more women feel justified in disrespecting all men they come into contact with. And sadly, these are the very same women who end up single, with many children and even more emotional baggage. Leave these bitter and future "hags" alone.

Keep a close eye on the language she uses. Does she constantly test your manhood? Will she call you a "punk"? It's one thing to joke with someone, but if she is a little too comfortable with disrespectful language it needs to be addressed swiftly. And if it continues, you must cut her off. Continuing to deal with a disrespectful woman subtlely communicates to yourself, that you don't deserve any better. Do not put yourself in this type of relationship.

Multiple Baby Daddy Women

If you're considering getting with a woman who has multiple children by various men, you need to seriously reevaluate your dating choices. The dating pool on Twitter isn't *that* bad. While these types of ladies might be nice and well-intentioned, having multiple children without any sort of commitment to the father is a bad move. Among other things, it shows a lack of sound judgment. If she can't be serious about the father of her children, do NOT take HER serious either. Leave women who have kids all "willy-nilly" alone.

Although I've personally dealt with a female who lied about her children, women typically do not deny having children. If you don't know how many she has, then it's cool to ask. As you get to know her, you can probe a little deeper. In most circumstances, I would not consider dating a woman with more than one child.

Long Distance Women

Back when I was new to online dating, I made this error time and time again. I would hope to magically meet someone from far away and date her. But let's be real—at *best*, long distance relationships are hard. And without a solid face-to-face foundation, long distance relationships are nearly impossible. Plus, unless you are holding some serious cash, the chances that your wallet can sustain the cost to travel across the state, or even the country is unlikely. When on Twitter, aim to only pursue women who are within a reasonable distance. There are some exceptions, namely if you are "vacation mackin". More on that later. You can tell where she is, usually by her profile. If not, simply ask.

Underage Women

No, no and no. I do not condone statutory rape. Only interact with women who are of legal age. If you are in the U.S. the "safe" age is 18. If you stick to that rule, you'll be fine.

To avoid young chicks, be on the look out for the following:
1. Girls who make fish faces in their profile
2. Girls who tYp3 lyKE th1S
3. Girls who use terms like **lolz**, **bff**, and **okie**
4. Girls who wear an extraordinary amount of pink

If you avoid these rules, do not blame me if you end up on the new season of Dateline NBC's, "To Catch a Predator".

TWOBABLIES

Chubby Chelseas

In spite of what many might say, choosing to date a big girl is more than just a preference. More often than not, people tend to become overweight and obese due to not getting enough exercise and/or poor eating habits. Furthmore, those who are overweight are more likely to develop diseases.[6] With that said, anyone who is not actively trying to keep their weight in check suffers from a lack of discipline and it is *this* that you should be weary of. Others gain weight as a result of stress or while dealing with trauma. One should love life more than food.

So when it comes to dating an overweight woman, remain cautious. Is she dealing with any psychological issues? Is she actively trying to control her weight? Is she disciplined? Does she care about her appearance? These are all important questions to ask yourself.

---

[6] Author: Unknown. "Obesity Information". American Heart Association. http://www.heart.org/HEARTORG/GettingHealthy/WeightManagement/Obesity/Obesity-Information_UCM_307908_Article.jsp. Last Updated: 01/20/2011.

Attention Seekers

More than Facebook and even MySpace (in its prime), Twitter is notorious for the number of attention whores. As society becomes more sexualized so do social networks. And Twitter is an attention whore's paradise.

It's never a challenge to identify a classic Attention Whore on Twitter because she makes it her *mission* to be seen. This is multiplied tenfold when sexually suggestive trending topics enter the mix. For instance, on Thursdays, a popular Trending Topic is #thongthursdays. Virtually every attention whore posts photos of herself wearing a thong, hoping to gain attention and followers. Another popular tending topic is #tittytuesdays. I'll let you fellas guess what's on the agenda on those days.

Tread lightly with these women. They aren't in the red category because these women *can* be approached and macked on. However, they should not be taken seriously. If a woman is an attention whore, she's basically telling you that she's not done seeking sexual attention from guys. This is why many of these same women are on YouTube shaking ass.

Vain Women

Why is this in the "Twobablies" category? Well, if you're looking for a girlfriend, stay away from vain women altogether. However, if you're just looking for a physical encounter or two, then there's no harm in attempting to get at her. Vain women only care about themselves. They are the type that never ask you about your day, how you're doing, or what you like to do. Many of these women have no problem standing up guys on dates, and never bother to talk to anyone unless it directly benefits them. Vain women make up the majority of groupies in society, so this is why these women are only good for temporary, physical relationships. *Never* take this woman seriously or allow her access to your love life or you will end up losing.

Telling if a woman is vain on Twitter is simple. Just look for one word…"ME". If her timeline is about how good she looks or how she's so "great", then she's vain. If every other tweet is a link to her photographing herself, she's vain. If her twitter background contains a collage of her modeling photos, and her showing off her sexual body parts, she's vain!

Models, Strippers, and Porn Actresses

While I want all of you guys to aim high, there are some things you should realize about models, strippers and porn stars. For one, most of these women receive hundreds of messages from men (and women) in a very short period of time. The prettier she is (or the more skin she shows), the larger her audience. With these women, my advice is to find ways to stand out. The last thing you should do is fall into the trap of complimenting her on her beauty. You don't want to be her *fan*. Watch what she tweets about and look for an opening, preferably while she's online. The more creative your reply is, the more likely she is to respond. And if your profile information and photo is in order, she may respond.

Yet, if she has over 10,000 followers, your chances of being noticed are smaller. In any event, do not act like a "bug-a-boo" and sweat this woman. Always keep your dignity above your desires and move on if she doesn't reply. Perhaps a month or two down the line, you can try again.

"Barbies" and "Gagas"

With the advent of Lady Gaga and hip hop superstar Nicki Minaj, a lot of women are adopting very eccentric and frankly odd personas. Nicki Minaj fanatics refer to themselves as "barbies". Like the Barbie Doll character, these women usually die or bleach their hair white or pink and apply a "cakeload" of makeup. Lady Gaga fanatics are a bit harder to describe, but easier to point out. These women are identified for dressing extremely odd—oversized shoulder pads, strangely cut dresses and shirts and odd makeup are a few of the signs.

While harmless in many cases, be on the lookout for "fakeness". Women who choose to reinvent themselves within a pop cultural theme are *literally* followers. While this is normally something teenage girls go through, there are many women who are well into their adult years still attempting to be a celebrity. There's not much guesswork to identify a Lady Gaga "Monster" or Nicki Minaj "Barbie". Just look for dyed hair and odd clothing. She shouldn't be hard to spot.

Bloggers

Honestly, I debated on whether to keep this type of woman in the *Twobablies* or place her in the *Twitches* category. The problem with female Bloggers is that any failed relationship or even a failed attempt to get to know her could lead to a *major* windfall, especially if she's popular. Twitter has given rise to a few celebrity bloggers, some with significantly large followings. For instance, celebrity blogger "Necole Bitchie" (@necolebitchie) has over 100,00 followers. Imagine the devastation a well-known blogger could create if you happen to get on her bad side. Exactly. Fellas, tread very lightly with bloggers—especially relationship bloggers. To be on the safe side, I would avoid them altogether unless you're advanced in your game.

Addicts

This category is one of the fastest growing categories of women on Twitter. When I say "addicts", I don't mean drug or sex addicts…necessarily. I'm talking about women with addictive and even obsessive personalities. Some women are obsessed with attention and celebrities, while others are obsessed with self-loathing and sending hateful messages. Not to mention the sex addicts and weed smokers.

What's ironic, is that society often places the focus on the substance or acts that are addictive, rather than the personality of the addict. For instance, I've heard many people say that Twitter is addictive when talking about persons who are on the site 24/7. However, if that were the case, why isn't *everyone* addicted to Twitter? The reason is because addiction depends, first and foremost, upon having an addictive personality.[7]

The danger in an "addict", is that her symptoms may be subtle and seemingly very gradual. For instance, I met a female online who seemed a bit sexual, but over time she became a full-blow sex addict. While it was very nice at first, there were times when she would call in the middle of the night, begging and pleading for sex. This would happen even if we had sex, just hours prior. It can get annoying and is a major turn off. With that said, be on the look out for what women *say* on Twitter. Look at her timeline and see what she talks about. My best advice is, if you choose to get to know this type of woman, make sure you proceed cautiously!

Single Mothers

Before I get into this, I will make a disclaimer: there's *nothing* wrong with mothers, nor is there anything wrong with children. After all, I have a mother and I used to be a child. This purpose of placing mothers in the "Twobablies" category is to point out the potential pitfalls of dating one.

---

[7] Mason, Stephen. "The Addictive Personality." Psychology Today. 3/14/09.

One drawback is the child's father. In some cases, he may be a good guy, or perhaps he's married to another woman. On the flipside, he could be in jail or even hiding in her bushes stalking her. In this case, your attempt to get to know a "M.I.L.F." could be downright dangerous!

Secondly, the child is also a major consideration. Personally, I have never seriously considered dating a woman who has children. While many single mothers say, "I'm not looking for a father for my child," you must consider what will happen if you two date or marry. Are you ready to be an important father figure in her child's (or children's) life? Also consider that you will always come second to her child.

Lastly, many single mothers carry a certain degree of baggage with them. This is somewhat understandable, especially if she feels abandoned by her child's father. If that's the case, she may have attachment issues—therefore even physical relationships (booty calls) should be monitored carefully. On that note, if you pursue a physical relationship with a single mother, do not see her more than once a week and keep phone calls to a minimum, or she will likely become very attached.

---

http://www.psychologytoday.com/blog/look-it-way/200903/the-addictive-personality

Long Distance Women

As opposed to my other books, I do not necessarily suggest avoiding women who live far away. While I always prefer to contact women in my general vicinity, Twitter is a cool PR Tool (Public Relations). Unlike other sites where conversations and exchanges are generally private, most of the dialogue on Twitter is *public*. Therefore, flirting with "fly" women can help your game with local women. And since there is very little effort in contacting someone (just a simple update), then why not show off your "mackin" skills? And if either one of you lives near a popular destination, then there's a possibility of crossing paths. One of my favorite vacation spots is Toronto, Canada. Therefore, I stay in touch with many of the local women in that area to ensure a group of ladies to hang out with while I'm there. On the flipside, I have personally met women from Twitter who've happened to travel to New York.

To identify a woman who lives far away, her location may be in her profile. Users who utilize GPS tracking applications like "Ubertwitter" to access Twitter on their mobile phones may also have their latitude and longitude listed on their profile. These numbers can pinpoint a person's location within 100 feet in some cases. It may list something like, "34.838521,-87.325974".

To figure out where this is, go to http://maps.google.com and paste the latitude and longitude numbers in there. (Just don't show up at her front door unannounced. That is creepy).

TWEETHEARTS

Career Women

One of my favorite women to talk to online are women with careers. Generally, these women are cool, easy to talk to, and have jobs to support themselves. As opposed to women that are broke, career women have the ability to take *you* out or go dutch. And in these cases, you will not have to wonder whether she is only hanging around you to drain your pockets.

An added benefit to these women is the possibility that she's a freak. As I mentioned in my previous books, women who are in strict professions (such as teachers or police officers) tend to be the biggest sexual freaks. Don't say I didn't warn you!

Local Women

It is crucial to your game that you spend your time strategizing on how to locate women in your local area. A good way to organize locals is to create lists. For instance, if you live in Atlanta, you should periodically search on the hashtag phrase **#atlanta** or **#ATL**. There are also other things Atlanta is known for—landmarks, towns and counties, colleges, etc. Searching on any of these phrases will land you *dozens* of results. Next, create a list with the name "ATL" and add women who indicate they live in Atlanta to that list. Then when you log into Twitter, you will have the ability to sift through the women who live in your area. This will allow you to meet her *quickly* without the worry of packing your bags. More on "speed tweeting" in Chapter 7.

College Women

Whether or not you're in college doesn't make a difference—college women are very cool and easy to get with on Twitter. For one, locating them is a breeze. Locating school names and school mascots makes it easy to find women who go to those schools. Another tactic to locate these women is to find an official twitter page of the college. You will be able to view its followers and who it follows, which will undoubtedly contain many women.

Breaking into a dialogue with this woman is relatively easy as well. Simply asking her about her college experience, or commenting on something she's talking about is all it normally takes.

Military Women

I mistakenly forgot to mention military women in my past books, but I did not want to forget them in this one! I have personally met and dated military women from the net and had great experiences. One woman I met back in the day (back when MySpace was popular) had just come back from Iraq. She was so grateful to be back in her home town that she treated me like a king. She paid for our dates and let me borrow her car (mine was in the shop). On top of that she was extremely horny, given it had been months since she "got any". And on that note, keep in mind that women in the military are usually very fit. And fellas, this has its advantages!

Whatever type of woman you desire, make sure she's cool all around—especially if you're looking for a girlfriend. Too much of one thing is never a good thing. Now that you've found some fly ladies, it's time to figure out how to start things off!

chapter four – contacting her for the first time

By this time, you should have a good idea of what type of woman you are potentially contacting. Yet, if you cannot be effective in getting her attention, you will not be successful on Twitter.

I've personally noticed that peoples' attention spans seem much shorter—even as recent as four years ago. While it was normal to carry on a MySpace interaction for weeks, the success rate for meeting women off Twitter seems to deteriorate at a much faster pace. Thanks to the constant updates from the dozens or even hundreds of the people she's following, you're ability to get her attention is vital to your success rate.

What NOT To Do

Those who are familiar with my other books should already know what I am about to say. Fellas, under no circumstance should you compliment a woman's physique in your attempt to get her attention! This almost always fails as a woman does not respect a man she can control with her looks. Yes, most women certainly appreciate the attention. In fact, Twitter is jam-packed with women seeking attention for their appearance. And the more attractive she is, you can bet that she receives hundreds of compliments a day. When you compliment a woman's physique—especially a "sexual body part" like her breasts or her hips, she will likely view you as a fan, rather than a guy she could see herself meeting. Women love a *challenge*. Where's the challenge in statements like this?

"I want to rub baby oil all on that ass"

"I'd love to ride those curves"

"Wow, look at those titties! Can I squeeze?"

Saying things like this on Twitter place you in a subservient light. It shows that you value her physique over your pride. This *repels* women from you. Always talk to women as your equal. And if she's a little cocky, it is okay to talk *down* to her, at times.

Now that that's out of the way, there are two main approaches to opening up a conversation with a woman on Twitter. The approach you use depends on the type of woman she is. Here we go!

The Smooth Approach

In my experiences, this approach will work on the majority of the women in the *Tweethearts* category listed in the previous chapter.

The Smooth Approach is accomplished by "blending" into her timeline, then turning the tables into a one-on-one dialogue. There are various ways to do this; yet, the whole idea is to appeal to her ego to a certain degree. When people tweet, they feel good knowing that someone appreciated what they said and offered feedback. For instance, if a woman says that she's listening to a particular song, you can reply, saying she has a good taste in music and follow up with a statement or a question about her musical choice. This approach is smooth as you appear genuine.

Another approach is to provide an answer to her question, in a creative way. For example, over a year ago, I got in contact with a very attractive media personality on Twitter after she tweeted, "I'm at a whole foods supermarket right now. What should I cook for dinner?" I immediately replied to her, "BONE-SUCKIN' SAUCE…you need that in your life." She immediately replied to ask more questions about the item and ended up following me. Soon thereafter she and I began Direct Messaging (DM'ing) each other and exchanged contact information. A few months later, I interviewed on her show! This was another smooth way of getting to know her, as I provided a creative solution to her problem.

All in all, the aim of *The Smooth Approach* is to disarm her and get her to see you as a cool person. Most women are keenly aware that you probably want to have sex with them already. Keep her guessing.

The BOLD Approach

The second approach you can use on Twitter is to send a bold message to a female. This technique is not a perfect science, but it is necessary to get at certain females—especially attention-whores. Before I continue, I am going to caution you fellas that your results may be mixed until you get this right. You must realize that saying the *same* thing to two women may get you *completely different* results. In my experience, it's similar to trying to hit a home run. Certain pitches are easier to hit out of the park. You simply have to recognize which pitch is the home run ball. If you make contact on the right pitch, or lady, then a home run is inevitable!

I've successfully used this approach on many women. I suggest saving this tactic for women who are way above average in the looks department and seek male attention by flaunting their looks. For instance, if she changes her twitpic multiple times per week, shows off her breasts or booty all over her timeline, and tweets sexually suggestive things, then this approach is for her.

It's also best to be bold when you only have a small window of opportunity. Most often, this approach is best used for a potential sexual fling. This is because most attention whores are very emotionally unavailable and detached.

To be bold, you should say something that "jolts" her attention. Think about it—most guys who tweet her are being overly nice in their attempt to "woo" her. Therefore, being somewhat disagreeable, sarcastic, somewhat cocky and witty is what you should aim to achieve. At least initially. For example, if she invites her followers to comment on her appearance by saying, "How do you think I look?", you can reply with, "B-. Not bad, I guess :)". (Using the sideways smiley face emoticon adds a playful element to your reply).

Choosing the right approach depends on the woman and the situation. If she lives relatively close by, seems laid back, and doesn't have a lot of followers, "The Smooth Approach" is usually best. If say, you're in her area for a short period of time (a vacation) or she's in your area, "The Bold Approach" may be best. You don't have time for the polite introductions in this case. Sometimes you just have to swing for the fences. However in either instance, she will keep the conversation going if interested.

Friends of Co-workers

As you recall from Chapter 3, one of the *Twitches* you should stay away from is the co-worker. However, you *should* aim to get at her friends. In a way, this is an "inside track", since she is more likely to trust you since you work with her friend. So how do you get the conversation going? Peep game.

Say she is having an exchange with one of her friends. For instance, let's say your co-workers Twitter name is @coworker and her friend's Twitter name is @cutefriend. You could Tweet something like,

"@coworker I didn't know you had friends :) Who's @cutefriend? She seems interesting."

There are a few techniques used in this message. First, saying to @coworker, "I didn't know you had friends", is a sarcastic, humorous line and is effective in getting her attention. Second, saying "Who's @cutefriend? She seems interesting" lets @cutefriend know you're checking her out. However, unlike most guys who've probably tweeted her, you're not brown-nosing. You didn't say she was "beautiful" or "sexy". You said she was "interesting". On top of all that, you come off very confident since you publicly stated your interest. After saying this, it is up to @coworker or even @cutefriend to reply. If it is favorable, you've been chosen!

Trending Topics and Hashtags

As described in Chapter 2, finding women through hashtag keywords or Trending Topics can be very effective. Once you find a woman you'd like to get to know, what do you say to her? For one, use the knowledge you already have. For instance, if you found her through a search on #Brooklyn, you can proceed to ask a question or make a comment about Brooklyn.

This is even more effective with Trending Topics because of the exposure. For instance, one of my favorite shows on television are the re-runs of MSNBC's "To Catch A Predator". While internet predators are a very serious matter, it is somewhat comical to see the lengths these men go through to meet underage teens for sex. That said, #TCAP (To Catch A Predator), tends to "trend" highly while it airs. To add to the mix, if I see an attractive woman commenting on the show, I'll tweet, #CuteChickOnTCAPtimeline @HerName. While this is certainly not a direct approach, it accomplishes two things: 1) She will notice you, and 2) so will everyone else, which will increase your following, if done correctly. As I always say, nothing gets a woman's attention like *other* women!

chapter five – Sealing the deal and taking it offline

This chapter is where "the rubber meets the road" and is perhaps one of the most important chapters in the book. Moreover, this is where most other "internet dating guides" fail, as they do not adequately explain how to quickly and efficiently move an interaction offline. So how do you get her *off* Twitter? First you have to take action and stop what's hindering you. The first step is to get rid of your fears.

Too many men fail to act upon their goals for dating. This is due to a fear of rejection. A trusted and popular website, AskMen.com has a series of articles which addresses this fear and gives guys tips on how to overcome it. This fear is defined pretty well here:

...there is one natural fear that seems to overshadow most men: the fear of rejection. This instinctive emotion paralyzes and hinders us from doing the things we really want to do, including meeting women. Some men are so afraid of rejection that they would rather run through a minefield than walk up to a woman and ask her out on a date.[8]

Unfortunately, there are many guys who are so uncomfortable about the idea of failing, that they would rather remain alone.

---

[8] Smith, Curt. "Overcome Your Fear of Rejection". AskMen.com. Obtained Jan. 17, 2011. http://www.askmen.com/dating/curtsmith/19_dating_advice.html

You need to do your best to keep these guys at a distance when you are working on *your* game. They will try to discourage you, as every success you achieve will remind them of how inferior, or "whack" they are. They are the types of guys that say:

"She'll never go out with a guy that she met online!"
"She's a celebrity…she'll never talk to me!"
"She probably has a boyfriend."
"I'm not talking to her. She's probably a hooker."
"She's out of my league."

Fellas, words are powerful so you need to do your best to stay around like-minded individuals. This extends to the world of business as well. If you want to be rich, hang around rich people. If you want to be a mack, hang around other macks. Adopting a certain mindset depends upon the messages and people you surround yourself with. I say all this because you will *never* get anything out of this book until you make the commitment that you will not allow your fears to stop you. Always keep learning from your mistakes, use this book as your wingman, and keep it moving!

The Three D's

Now that you are ready to face your fears head on, you must also have a plan. Your plan for meeting women off Twitter is to accomplish the Three D's.

Here are the Three D's of Meeting Women off Twitter:

1. **D**ialogue
2. **D**ialing
3. **D**ating

Dialogue

One of the most common questions I receive from guys is, "How do I keep the conversation going with a woman online?" It's very tough answering this because it's not the correct question to ask. Instead, he should be asking *how* to converse with her. He should also keep in mind his goal which is, again, to meet her *off* Twitter.

When people think of a "dialogue", many assume that this is a long drawn out conversation that could take a lot of time—perhaps days or even weeks. Absolutely not. On Twitter, your goal is to have her call you within two to three days from the first point of contact. There are varying factors which makes it acceptable for this to happen within a week or so, like if she doesn't tweet often, or if neither of you are online at the same time. Yet, life is too precious if you spend weeks on end trying to meet a woman off Twitter.

Once you've caught her attention (using the rules given in Chapter 4), your next three or four messages will typically be "mentions". A mention is anything that alerts them you're talking to them on the public timeline. The goal of the "First D" (dialogue) is for you two to follow each other so your conversation can be private. Private messaging on Twitter is called "Direct Messaging".

The content of your dialogue will vary. However, as opposed to my previous books, my advice is to keep things much more "light" on Twitter, due to the openness of the site. The public timeline is viewable to any and everyone, so you must always be tactful. I have routinely seen men who've made overly bold approaches to women on the public timeline, only to be rejected or worse—have the woman laugh at and share his comment with others. In fact, just last week, a lady I know shared a tweet a guy sent her, stating that he needs my help. In a way, I felt bad for him. However, she should know better than to air out his "holleration" attempts for the world to see.

So what do you say? Using our example from Chapter 4, let's say you searched on #Brooklyn, and found a female who tweeted that she recently moved to Brooklyn. Your initial tweet could be, "I saw that you're new to NY. We love out of towners. Don't get robbed ;)" Most likely she'll respond positively. Why? It was original. You didn't use a pick up line. Plus, it was a bit comical. The "tip off" was the "wink" emoticon at the end. Always use this when there's a chance she could misinterpret your message. If her response is something short, like "I'll try not to", then she's probably not interested. At this point you could still ask her how she likes New York. If she responds favorably and asks you something about yourself, this is a *green light* so act accordingly. However, if she keeps her answers short and abrupt, move on.

Here's an example of a winning dialogue:

YOU: @CuteGirl *I saw that you're new to NY. We love out of towners. Don't get robbed ;)*

HER: @You *LOL I'll try not to. So far everyone's been nice, but it's so much colder than California!*

YOU: @CuteGirl *People tend to be meaner too! Hopefully you're at least SOMEWHAT nice :)*

HER: @You *Of course! Where in the city are you from?*

YOU: @CuteGirl Harlem. I can actually see Yankee Stadium from my window.

HER: @You Cool. I've never been up there.

YOU: @CuteGirl Hmm, well if you play it right, maybe we'll see. By the way, follow me. I want to DM you something.

Fellas, these are the types of conversations you want. Your conversations won't always go as planned and that's okay. As a mack, your goal isn't to be a fortune teller. Your goal is to be able to smoothly handle every and any potential challenge. (I will talk about these in the next chapter). Just remember to never try to persuade her into gaining more interest. If she isn't responding favorably, then move on!

Dial

Once you've established a good public dialogue your goal is to get her to "DM" or Direct Message you so you can exchange phone numbers (or give her your number). Your DM dialogue should be relatively short—no more than six exchanges. Your final DM should invite her to call you. Most women are somewhat fearful or hesitant about getting to know men online. Disarm that feeling by having comfortable conversation. To do this, get into her world. Have her tell you about herself. Then, give her a tactful compliment and leave your number.

Here's a sample DM chat (from our earlier conversation):

[In the Direct Message]

HER: Hi :)

YOU: Hello. You seem like a cool female. So what do you do for fun? Done anything exciting since moving to Brooklyn?

HER: Not yet :(I've been buried in school work. Maybe sometime soon.

YOU: Really? What are you studying? Sounds challenging!

HER: Chemical Engineering! Yeah, it's pretty tough. I'm surprised all my hair isn't gray!

YOU: Maybe gray is your color! Lol. But seriously, that's too bad! Well if you're as cool as you seem, maybe we'll hang out ;)

HER: You're funny! I like that. Okay maybe.

YOU: Hey, I gotta run. Call me tonight around 8. 555-555-5555 (John)

HER: Okay. 555-555-7777. Amy

In case you were wondering, a tactful compliment is something I referred to earlier in this book in the "Bold Approach" section. Try using wit, charm, and a slight air of "friendly cockiness" to win her over. In the previous DM example, the quote, "maybe gray is your color" was more witty than anything. A friendly-cocky approach might be, "well, you're not bad looking for a nerdy girl ;)" Knowing how to talk to her depends on her type, per our breakdown in Chapter 3.

Here's the simple rule with phone calls. It is ideal that she calls *you*. Why? She already knows that you like her. After all, you approached her. So if you leave your number and she calls you at your requested time, her interest in you is at a good level. If she calls later, her interest in you is likely proportional to the amount of time she took to reach out to you. And if she never calls, she probably wasn't interested. In most cases, women will never tell you how they feel. They will show you. Texting doesn't count either. If she texts you after you asked her to call you, politely direct her to call you. Simply put, texting is not good enough, so don't accept this in place of phone calls. If she texts you, she might as well continue to DM you. If she likes you *enough*, she'll find a way to call.

As I've repeatedly advised in my other books, keep phone calls short and sweet, especially the first call. Your objective should be clear with every first phone chat—to schedule a date, or a time to "kick it". The first call should last no longer than 10-15 minutes. Do not discuss religion or politics this soon either. Use this time to elaborate what you two have already discussed online. Using our previous example, you can ask her how she got into Chemical Engineering, what her talents are, and what life is like in California. That by itself should take ten minutes. Below the surface this time is important because she will feel like she knows you. This will increase the odds of her going out with you. However extending the phone call beyond fifteen minutes will only hurt you. Why? Because by this point she knows all she needs to know to feel safe enough to hang out with you. And long conversations will only give her reasons *not* to go out with you.

At the end of your chat, preferably when the chat is still upbeat (to keep her wanting more), excuse yourself from the phone but tell her it was nice talking to her. Suggest that you two should hang out and propose a time, day and activity. If she doesn't completely accept, have her call you when she's ready. Then let her go. However, if she accepts, proceed to the date.

Dating

Congrats, you've made it to the date! Even if your goal is to have a physical relationship, I normally still call it a "date", although some guys don't use that word. In any event, make sure that your hygiene, your clothing and your confidence is top notch. In fact, if you're not experienced with dating, I suggest going above and beyond to make sure that you're confident when going out with this female. You can use this time to wear your new or less used clothes, polish your shoes, or get your hair trimmed.

My preferred places for a "first date", regardless of my intentions, are coffee shops, book stores, parks, museums and botanical gardens. Each of these places are inexpensive and make it easier to hold a conversation. If a woman is more interested in meeting you, rather than the money in your wallet, she will gladly accept. I have definitely had my share of women flatly reject my invite, because they wanted to be fed. Fellas, do not feed the "birds". Do not make a first date into an expensive romantic excursion. If she does well on your first one or two dates, then a lunch or dinner is acceptable.

For my fellas who just want sex, you must first understand that this is okay! Society and even many women will act as if desiring sex is a bad thing. Ironically many of these women are actively having sex with guys—many of whom they've only known for a few days, if that! If you meet a woman on Twitter and your goal is to only have a sexual relationship, simply be upfront about your desires. However, you need to be tactful.

Here are some good phrases to convey that you just want to "smash":

"I don't want anything serious"

"I'm just looking for friendship"

"I don't see myself being in a relationship anytime soon"

Remain unapologetic and you will be amazed at how many women will be fine with your straightforwardness. Never lead a woman down the wrong path by making her believe you are committed when you really aren't. Too many men do this and it always bites them in the end. Being a Mack and a "True-To-The-Game Player" means to always maintain your integrity and honesty.

Above all, remain confident on your date. This will shine through and will help with whatever your goals are.

chapter Six - Major twitfalls

I know that many of you are anxious to use the information given to you in the first five chapters to meet women off Twitter. In fact, I'm sure that many of you will be successful. However, this chapter will place an emphasis on the things that you should *not* do in your quest to be a "Twitter Mack" and this information should not be ignored. While studying Twitter over the past several months, I noticed that most guys were doing the same things which might cause most women to turn the other way. Fellas, women are very perceptive beings. Doing or tweeting something that might seem minor to you could be a major deal-breaker for her!

Here are the five things you should avoid *at all costs* on Twitter:

1. Randomly asking other Twitter users to follow you
2. Giving too much information about your personal life
3. Having Twitter arguments on your public timeline
4. Being a groupie
5. Being too available

Randomly asking others to follow you

Unless you know someone or have been conversing with a lady, as described in Chapter 5, do not ask other users to follow you. Asking someone on Twitter to follow you is like begging for money. That's because while some people will feel bad and do it, you are more of a nuisance than anything else. It makes you look lame.

Most people who've asked me to follow them back are starving rap artists and amateur models. For the most part, they've had under 200 followers and are following way more people than are following back. After getting someone's mention which says, "Hey follow me!", I may look at their timeline to see what they're talking about. Nine times out of ten, they're timeline shows that they've tweeted the same exact thing to dozens of others. Who wants to follow someone who begs for followers all day?

This hurts your game because you have no idea who is looking at your public timeline. Plus, if you've done this in the past, any woman you're currently trying to get to know may (and probably will) look back into your timeline to see what you've written. While having a significant following will give you a certain degree of "rock stardom", it's not something that should be asked for. It is earned. If you desire more followers you can either follow more people, or become more popular in the real world. Whatever the case, stay away from the public requests.

Giving too much information about your personal life

All too often, I'll see both men and women who post their life stories on Twitter. Most tweets should never be put out there. The main reason this should be avoided is because it takes away a key element that women find attractive: mysteriousness!

Women *love* mysterious men. Why? Well we often want what is not readily available to us. Most men give away their mystery, especially on Twitter. Here's an excellent snippet from an article in the *Examiner* on being mysterious:

We all know why Dan Brown's "The Da Vinci Code" was such a big success: it was attractive to many because it had the all-important quality of mystery.

Mystery is not only attractive in movies and novels. It is an important code for attracting women. A man of mystery is unpredictable in a good way. He exudes an air that makes women wonder what he is up to, or what he's going to do next. A man of mystery uses vague language in communicating his interest to women. He comes across as cool and challenging to women, and women love challenges.

If you want to exhibit this attribute, you need to develop a "leave it or take it" attitude that communicates to women that you don't need to attract them. This means acting in a cool way without a deliberate attempt to attract women. You don't want to present the image of a desperate "woman hunter". That will certainly get you nowhere. Women can sense when a man is desperate, and that is a turn-off. Being nonchalant and sometimes ignoring really hot women even when every other guy is giving her all their attention, is oftentimes what gets you noticed as different and challenging. And as noted earlier, women like challenges, and will be attracted to you just when you show them you don't care much about their beauty.[9]

When tweeting, always have something somewhat meaningful or entertaining to say. Letting your followers know every time you go to the bathroom, go to the store, do laundry, etc. will ruin your game. Also, avoid things which might give you a negative perception, like your alcohol addiction, recent breakups or your fascination with big breasted women. Less is always more. You don't need to over tweet in order to get ladies online. Got it? Good.

Having Twitter arguments on your public timeline

Avoid online drama at all costs. While you might see a temporary spike in your following from people who love drama, this will also put a bullet in your game. Most arguments are petty so no matter the reason, "Twitter Beefs" look very immature. No one cares who's "right" as arguing with anyone will always make you "wrong". If anything, take the argument offline and argue over the phone or in person. And if you don't know that person well enough to get this information, then any argument at all is pointless!

Being a groupie

This is not only a problem—it's an epidemic. Here's why: on any given stripper's Twitter profile she may literally have hundreds and even thousands of followers. Internet models also command a huge following on average. Many of these women aren't even serious models. However, guys from coast to coast and all over the world follow these internet models and attention whores. Many guys praise their beauty and look for ways to get to know her. The overwhelming majority of these guys fail because they are fans and groupies. And it is unnatural for a

---

[9] Boateng, Vincent. "The secret code for attracting women". DC Men's Relationship Advice Examiner. Dec. 23, 2010. http://www.examiner.com/men-s-relationship-advice-in-washington-dc/the-secret-code-for-attracting-women?render=print

woman to be attracted to a fan, especially if he praises her beauty.

Another thing many men do is agree with everything a woman says. Stop retweeting everything a cute woman says, just because she's cute. This also makes you an internet groupie. While an occasional retweet is cool, your goals is to have women follow and retweet you. If this isn't happening, you should make it a point to find interesting things to say and do.

Being too available

Always being available is yet another way you will damage your game online. One thing you must try not to do is respond to everyone so quickly—especially women. With the advent of dozens of Twitter applications popping up on smartphones, ipads, and the like, it is very easy to have real time access to Twitter. The instant one "tweets" you, it is easy to be notified in real time. Do not fall victim to the temptation of responding to cute women so quickly!

Being so accessible gives off an air of desperation. And similar to giving out too much information on your timeline, being too accessible takes away your mysterious vibe. At the very least, do not respond to women quicker than they respond to you. Always make women work for your time and attention. She will appreciate you more.

With that said, onto one of my favorite concepts: "Speed Tweeting".

chapter seven – "speed tweeting"

Any topic having to do with speeding things up is my favorite because I am very impatient. I don't like waiting for things, especially when I know I am deserving of them. This includes meeting up with women.

Speed Tweeting is the act of bringing women from Twitter to an in-person meeting or "date" within 24 hours or much sooner. I've personally used this method, especially when I've been bored and wanted to meet a woman to hang out with *that day*. *Instant* gratification!

This chapter will put your skills to the test. If you think you're good, this chapter will either prove your worthiness or show where you need improvement. The goal is to enable you to go from a boring Saturday afternoon, to a fun-filled Saturday evening with the lady you *just* met on Twitter. In previous books, I talked about times where I've met women off social networking sites within thirty minutes. However, with Twitter, it is even possible to meet someone within *minutes* of seeing them online! Did I get your attention? Proceed.

There are two major ways of Speed Tweeting: *Conventional Speed Tweeting* and *Mobile Speed Tweeting*. Each has it's own advantages and choosing the one to use mostly depends on your geography (where you live), and your current location (whether at home, in a social setting, a networking event, etc.)

"CONVENTIONAL" SPEED TWEETING

The Conventional Method of Speed Tweeting is the slower of the two methods and is best used if you are at home and not out and about. This is however, the easier method to put to use since you will have more time to evaluate your next move. Your success rate will also likely be better since this method allows the woman to feel more justified in meeting you within a short period of time. Although we are well into the 21st Century, many women still feel conflicted about openly admitting to meeting men online. If speed tweeting is to be done, then "Conventional" Speed Tweeting is your key to getting more conservative women off Twitter quickly.

There are four basic steps to Conventional Speed Tweeting, as follows:

1. Find
2. Follow

3. Flirt (and have her follow you)

4. Finish

Target time to meeting her in person = 30 Minutes to 24 Hours

Find

The key to speed tweeting is to find women who are either currently online or at least women who use Twitter all the time. Because Twitter can be set up to alert users via text message, email, and through mobile applications, it is possible to speed tweet if someone isn't currently online at the moment. However, your best bet is to catch her live.

To find her, you'll want to search on a keyword as described in Chapter 2. Since your goal is to meet her in person within a short period of time, you should search on the name of your city, nearby landmarks, or anything having to do with your location. For example, if you live in Manhattan, you might search on the terms, "Manhattan", "Empire", "NYC", "Big Apple", "Broadway", and "Knicks". Doing this will land you many prospects, especially if you're near a large city. Once you *find* a woman who catches your eye, use the lessons in Chapter 3 to identify her type.

Follow

Simply stated, if the woman is in an acceptable category to you, "follow" her.

Flirt (and have her follow you)

Next, you must flirt. Your method can be similar to the "Seal the Deal" Chapter, but since she's currently online, you will have to turn this up. In this case, your goal is to have her follow you back within two tweets. Here's an example:

YOU: @*cutegirl That tweet was HILARIOUS. Most women from Houston are boring. You're not bad!*

HER: @*You Lol, thanks I try. Glad you liked it :)*

YOU: @cutegirl *Follow me. I want to DM you something*

The beauty of this approach is that she will not follow you if she's not interested. Also keep in mind that her following you does not *necessarily* mean she's into you. But if she doesn't follow after your attempt, take a break and move onto the next woman. (Keep in mind that you should not do this too many times in a row, as consistent rejections make you look bad to *your* followers).

When a woman is not interested, yet does not know how to reject you, she won't follow you, but will instead ask a question. From the example above, she might say:

HER: *@You What are you going to DM me?*

While this is a fair question, realize that her hesitancy is a sign that this conversation may not go well. You can reply and try to save it, by saying, "Follow and find out ;)" However, if she proceeds to ask more questions or doesn't follow you, then move on. Any hard-pressed attempt to get her to follow you will make you look *really* desperate. Once she follows you back, it's time to finish!

Finish

Once she follows you back, you should engage her in a quick Direct Message (DM) exchange and direct her to call you, right then and there. Your goal is to exchange less than four Direct Messages (DM's) at *most*. This is where you'll have to use your best judgment. If she's at home and seems to be relatively free, you don't have to be in a mad rush. However, if she's out of the house or is "on the move", your best bet is to handle this quickly.

Once you have her on DM, continue your previous conversation with her. From our previous example, here's an ideal conversation flow:

YOU: It's nice to know that ALL women from Houston aren't boring ;) So what area of the city are you from?

HER: Thanks :) I'm downtown, not to far away from the Hyatt.

YOU: Oh that's right up the road. You're actually not a bad looking woman. I'm John by the way.

HER: I'll take that as a compliment. LOL. I'm Lisa. Nice to meet you John.

YOU: What are you doing right now?

HER: Just finished my paper for class.

YOU: Call me right now: 555-5555

HER: Ok.

Nothing spectacular is needed. Wit and light comedy is okay, but don't go overboard. In addition, do not use Twitter to get to know her if you wish to meet her that day. This is where most guys come short. Save the "getting to know" for the phone and for the in-person meeting. *Speed* can be better achieved during a live conversation. Getting to know her on Twitter makes her get to know you as "that guy she met online", versus "that guy she got to know during the phone call or at the coffee shop.

If you notice in the above example, we don't poke *direct* fun at her (although this is acceptable if she's an attention whore). Yet, we do say, "It's nice to know that ALL women from Houston aren't boring ;)". This is a confusing, yet somewhat comical statement. For one, notice that it's not brown-nosing her or complimenting her beauty. Also while I suggest that most women from her city are boring, I say that she isn't. It's not a *true* compliment and that's what will get her attention. This is because most guys rely on outright compliments hoping it will get her to like him. However, *you* will have an air of being somewhat of a challenge and an independent thinker. This is what women want.

If she calls, this is an indication that she's interested in taking things further. If your approach was rocky, or if she stops messaging you, she's not interested *enough* to continue. That's okay—move on. Never try to *convince* a woman to like you.

During the phone call, you should again keep the conversation relatively short—no more than 20-25 minutes. Return to your

Twitter conversation and then get her to tell you all about herself. As I always say, the more she talks about herself, the more she'll feel comfortable around you! Here are some good questions to keep her talking:

-*What's your family like?* (Ask about her life growing up, where she lived, about her siblings, etc)

-*What are you currently doing with yourself? Work? School?*

-*What are your life goals? What do you want to do?*

-*What do you do for fun?*

To get her to talk more, always ask "how so?" or "why's that?" after the appropriate answers. Fellas, women love to talk—especially about themselves. After twenty or so minutes on the phone, set up a "date" or a time to "kick it" using the Dating guidelines in Chapter 5. If she's not receptive on the phone, learn to read between the lines and delete her number.

Now, if your goal is to meet her for sex, you have to take a couple of risks so that she's on the same page. Toward the end of the conversation (after 10-15 minutes), you need to guide the conversation into talking about physical things. A good transitional subject to use is "working out", because it involves the body. You can ask if she works out and what sorts of exercises she does. If she doesn't work out, you can ask her what she thinks her best physical features are.

Then, you can take a risk. You can ask something along the lines of,

"When was the last time you had sex?"

"Are you a freak?"

"How big is your booty?"

As you become more seasoned at "Twitter Mackin'", you will know far in advance whether she is down to "get down". And if she answers these questions with no hesitation, invite her to "kick it" with you at a public location. If she acts shocked at your question, **always act unapologetic and like everything you said is *totally*** normal. Most women act shocked because they do not want to appear promiscuous. Yet, this will turn some women off. In any event, you must remain unapologetic. Why? In my experiences, there have been many cases where women reject the direction of the conversation, but will later call me for some "action". I owe this to keeping it totally real. At the end of the day, who cares? And fellas, you would be surprised at the amount of women who will respect your boldness and will go along with it!

Once you meet her in person, take the time to get strike up a good conversation and invite her to your place (or her place) to watch a movie. From here, you should know what to do.

"MOBILE" SPEED TWEETING

Mobile Speed Tweeting is the champion of all champions. I estimate that less than 5% of guys will be able to do this successfully, as there is a certain amount of confidence and bravado involved. You must be bold, direct, and throw caution to the wind. The risks are big, but the rewards are vast. There's nothing like *meeting* her after one minute of *tweeting* her!

How is this possible? The key is that you must use your mobile device, like a smartphone, iPad or anything mobile with a Twitter application installed. With each passing day, more and more people utilize Twitter while out and about. There is no reason why you have do confine yourself to a home while internet dating!

The last time I used this technique, I met about five women at a popular party in Toronto, during their annual Caribana West Indian Festival. I was at a large party with over 5,000 party goers and used my Blackberry Smartphone to find some ladies. Now don't get me wrong—I was mackin' the regular way, as well. I was using eye contact, approaching women and doing it the "old-fashioned" way all night. But I also perfected the craft of getting them off Twitter. I'll get into my techniques in a moment.

There are only three steps to Mobile Speed Tweeting, as follows:
1. Find
2. Flirt
3. Find

Target time to meeting her in person = 1 to 30 Minutes

(First) Find

As opposed to the "Find" in the Conventional Section where you search on your city, your best bet is to search on your current *venue*. Recommended places are popular lounges, restaurants, sporting events, and museums. Each of these places are fun atmospheres, where you can easily meet a fly lady from Twitter.

One upscale lounge I frequent in New York City is called, "Pranna". During a big event, it is not uncommon to see hundreds of people using Twitter to talk about their experiences while at the venue. To use this to your advantage, you can search on the keyword, "Pranna" and find a woman you wouldn't mind kickin it with. In fact, it is okay to be greedy and find multiple women. After all it is a social event!

Flirt

While it sounds cliché, one of the best pieces of advice is to find women you have something in common with. That is what's on your side with Mobile Speed Tweeting. You and your twitchick are at the same venue at the same time! Therefore, your opening line can be something as innocent as, "Hey, I saw you mentioned Pranna. Any idea why they're not playing good music?" or "Why is this coat check line so long?" If she seems to be playful, you can even tweet her, "It's nice to know there are a few attractive ladies here tonight. Not bad ;)"

Whatever you tweet, make sure it doesn't sound doctored. Always be situational. If she likes the direction of the conversation, she'll message you back. Your goal is to meet her within three exchanges. If she doesn't initiate it, you can simply tweet, "Where are you right now? Hopefully you're as cute as you are in your pic. lol."

Find

This one should now be obvious. Once you two agree on a place to meet, *find* her. However this is key: don't go charging at her like a bat out of hell. Take your time. Flirt with *other* women along the way. Who knows…she might already be looking at you. I remember I met a woman at a basketball game on Twitter and she confessed that she was already checking me out before I messaged her. Your goal is to not only find her—but to make it look like you're doing her a favor. While it sounds sleazy, this will actually lower her defenses since many guys act like kiss-asses.

Once you two are in person, get to know each other. If she's with her girlfriends, you don't necessarily want to infiltrate. However, in some situations, you two can get to know each other and leave together. The world is truly yours!

chapter eight – getting at twitter celebrities

Given you've fully digested the advice given in the previous seven chapters, getting at Twitter celebrities should be simple. That's because it *is* simple, in concept!

So what is a Twitter Celebrity? I define a Twitter Celeb as anyone with more than 50,000 followers (especially those who only follow a small percentage of people). These are typically ladies who are famous singers, actresses, and models. Fellas, I'm not saying that this is the *easiest* type of woman to get at. Truthfully, the odds aren't in your favor. However, this chapter will give you your best shot!

Your goal is to be authentic and NOT to do what everyone else does. There are three techniques to getting this done, all of which I've put into good use over the past several months.

1. Give a suggestion
2. Treat her like someone you know
3. Knock her off her "high horse"

Give a suggestion
This one goes a long way. Most celebrities and notable people are very conscious about their appearance, their image, and the

way they do business. Singers are not only concerned with the sound of their music, but also their image in the public light. And fellas, you already know how insecure *regular* women are—multiply that tenfold with a celebrity twitchick!

Giving a Twitter celebrity a tactful suggestion can go a long way. While most guys are making an obvious attempt to get with her and compliment her, your suggestion will stand out as someone who's simply, "looking out" for her. A suggestion could be anything—yet it should be genuine. Not long ago, I did this with a popular radio personality. I tweeted her a suggestion that she should include some of her radio updates via audio on her Twitter timeline, as this is what people know her for. She immediately thanked me and has messaged me a few times since. Moreover, I gained a few dozen lady followers after I was showered with attention. Sounds like a win-win to me!

Whatever the suggestion, do not fall into the trap of sounding like a fan. Instead, act as if you're her friend or coach. And if she doesn't reply, let it go. While celebrities are not attracted to "fans", they file lawsuits against *stalkers*. Don't let it be you!

Treat her like someone you know

Treating her like someone you know is authenticity at its finest. Most celebrities do not need to be impressed by material things and status. Many guys believe that you cannot get with a celebrity unless you're a celebrity. Totally wrong. The reason why celebs typically hang around each other is because it's nothing to marvel over. Regular people tend to lose their damned minds when they meet a celebrity. Don't let this be you.

Don't overcomplicate this one. Pretend like she's a friend. An acquaintance. It can be as simple as saying "Good morning. How's life treating you?" You will be pleasantly surprised at the number of responses you'll get, especially if your profile is in order.

Knock her off her "high horse"

This is, by far, my favorite method of the three. The reason is that if it works, you are far more successful in the long run. The impact of telling it "like it is" with a celebrity usually makes a significant impact. She'll think about you. And depending on her level of insecurity, the benefits are huge.

There were a couple of models I consider *major* attention-whore's on Twitter, both of whom I met offline using this technique. In each case, I downplayed her appearance, directly.

While I do not remember all the details, one of them would constantly post photos of herself in skimpy attire. While most guys were flooding her with compliments, my responses were along the lines of "Ehhhhhhh" and "Not bad, I guess. Arch your back more." Or, "Good. B+." In most responses, I would include a smiley face so my message is viewed in good fun. In this case, she ate it up and we were in person within a week.

There's another model who I had a lengthy exchange with after I called her out for her desperate cry for attention. This one did not turn out so well, but it shows the power of "keepin' it real." She would post sexy photos, then would talk about how she hadn't had sex in months due to her pledge of celibacy. (Which is bullsh*t in most cases). Given her tens of thousands of male followers, she knew this would drive them crazy. Instead of going with the "flow of brown-nosing", I took the opposite approach. I told her to cut it out and pointed out that she probably isn't celibate at all. She immediately replied as if she had no idea what I was talking about. About twenty exchanges later, we were still going at it while I was gaining followers and of course, her attention. She paid absolutely no attention to the guys who were complimenting her and directed her emotions toward me.

While I never made a move to "get at her", our exchange showed the power of authenticity. What I said struck a chord because she was finally called out for her behavior. Although I no longer follow her updates, I have noticed that she has taken a much more conservative approach in her tweets, since our dialogue. As we discovered in Chapter 3, attention-whores are "Twobablies". She was a "Twobably-Not". Remember fellas, if she loves herself *too much* then your best bet is to leave her by herself.

chapter nine – organizing your "twitchicks"

You will need this chapter if you're successful with meeting women online. One of the biggest problems I had once I began to perfect the art of online dating was organizing the dozens, and eventually hundreds of women I met online. Anyone who knows me, knows that my memory sucks when it comes to names. And given that it was not uncommon for me to meet over 30 women in one month via the internet, this chapter isn't only necessary—it's vital!

A common technique to aid you in remembering who a woman is, is to use name-face association. This is done by mapping her face and her name, which is an effective way in remembering who she is.[10]

My simple, time-tested remedy is to use Microsoft Powerpoint, so you can effectively organize every woman you've met online—Twitter included. Within a few moments, you can recall everything you need to know about a female. Not only will it give you more confidence, but it will impress her . Here's how it's done:

Anatomy of a Powerpoint Slide

At the top of the slide should be her name and nickname, if she has one. The left side of the slide should contain her age, phone number, how you two met, her location and other facts that will aid in jogging your memory about her. On the right-hand side, include at least two photos so you can associate her name with her appearance. The graphic below demonstrates how this should look.

HER NAME

- AGE
- PHONE NUMBER
- HOW WE MET
- CITY (STATE)
- VIRGIN? FREAK?
- HEIGHT, WEIGHT, PHYSICAL FEATURES
- INTERESTING FACTS

Below every Powerpoint slide is a small section which says, "Click to add notes". This is where you have the option to paste

---

[10] Author: Unknown. "The Associative Method: Putting Names and Faces Together to Remember Better". The Psychologist World. Accessed: Jan 2011. http://www.psychologistworld.com/memory/association.php

an entire message exchange or chat. There have been situations where I'll forget damn near everything about a female and what we talked about. This section has saved me beyond measure! Take advantage of every Powerpoint slide and you'll be a more effective mack!

Keying her name in your phone

Imagine having six "Brittany's" and four "Tiffany's" in your phone. Welcome to my world. In this situation, not even Powerpoint will help you, especially if you are out on the road. And while a woman understands that many have the same name as her, no woman wants to be confused with another. That is why you need to be effective in differentiating between all your "Brittany's".

Fellas, I fully expect the majority of you to use Twitter to it's fullest potential, where it won't be out of the ordinary for you to meet at least one female off Twitter on a weekly basis. And odds are, you will inevitably find a few who share the same name. Here's how you should key their name into your phone.

First off, always spell her name correctly if she has a common name. For instance, if her name is "Tiffanee" rather than "Tiffany", spell it the way *she* spells it, simply because it is easy to remember who she is. The exception is women who have very unusual names that are hard to pronounce. In these cases, I always spell her name in a way that I have no problems pronouncing it when we speak on the phone. This *always* impresses women and will instantly give you a leg up.

Here are some examples of names you might see in my phone (these are slightly modified, so that I don't get angry phone calls from the women I know. lol):

Nikki Harlem Curly BB dimp
This is a woman named Nikki who's from Harlem, New York. Her hair was very curly on her Twitter photo, who has a big butt (BB). She also had a very pronounced dimple (dimp).

Brittany Miami 21 BlkDom Ins
This is a woman named Brittany that I met in Miami. She's 21 and is Black and Dominican (BlkDom). She also works in insurance (Ins).

Joo-Lee-Sah Julissa 24 PR prpmgr
This is a woman named Julissa, but pronounced her name like "Joo-Lee-Sah". Since I knew there was a good chance I'd mess up the pronunciation, I took the time to write it out the way I'd

say it. She's 24, is Puerto Rican (PR) and is a Property Manager (prpmgr).

Also keep in mind how well this technique works in nightclubs. Given that you are in a confined location for at least an hour, you can potentially meet many women. Unlike Twitter, you won't be able to store any photos—unless you take every woman's picture, which I do *not* recommend! Therefore, always use identifying words when storing her number. It will go a long way!

chapter ten – bonus tips

now we are at the final chapter. I have already given you enough tips to go out there are do some *serious* damage! However, I wanted to include a few more overall tips to make sure your game remains crisp.

Watch what you say

You must keep in mind that Twitter is a *community*. Unlike MySpace and Facebook, the *main* feature of Twitter are the status updates—not one-on-one interactions. Therefore, always monitor what you say and who it's directed toward. It is not difficult to dig back into someone's timeline and find out what they said weeks and even months ago. Even deleting your tweets isn't always effective as there are tools that can easily recover old tweets. Do not give into the temptation of slandering your ex or posting photos that you wouldn't want your mother to see. Doing this will usually bite you in the ass.

Never brown-nose

If you've learned nothing else from this book, learn *this*. Do not ever brown-nose a woman, thinking that this will bring you any closer to meeting her. Not only do overdone compliments never work, but they actually repel women from you. The prettier she is, the more brown-nosing compliments she receives on a regular basis. I cannot say this enough—the *more* you compliment her, the *less* she'll be attracted to you. Your independent mindset and confidence will do more for you in the long run than your compliments. While she might thank you for your words, she likely recognizes this as a pitiful attempt to get into her panties.

Don't overuse Twitter

Yes, I know this is a book on Twitter, but you have to know when to say when. It's cool to use Twitter on a daily basis, but not on an hourly basis. Like I mentioned earlier in the book, never message women back immediately, especially if she took a while to reply to your previous tweet. Never be too easily accessible as it gives you the appearance of seeming too "thirsty" or desperate.

Never argue online

Always take personal gripes offline or at least conduct them through private messages. Arguments will always hurt your game, whether it's with another man or woman. You will always come off looking better if you seem untouchable. Never allow personal matters to throw you off.

Timing is everything

One approach that has worked very well for me has been to contact women later in the evening, after 11:30PM local time. In most cases, user activity slows down and she is much less preoccupied with dozens of guys brown-nosing her. Most of the women I've met on the internet have been done around this time. Always swim downstream, along the path of least resistance. Late night tweets go a long way!

Find opportunities to DISagree

A little tension never hurt anyone. A healthy and semi-heated discussion may actually do wonders for your game. This technique is perhaps one of the advantages of Twitter, given that both your and her timeline are exposed to your exchange. And the more people who are involved in retweeting their responses and such, the more interesting you will become to her. Even better, if other women get involved, prepare for some subtle competition for your attention. Don't be afraid to speak your mind with an attractive female on Twitter!

CONCLUSION

Fellas, it was an absolute pleasure to write this book. I am completely confident that the advice given in this material will propel your game no matter which level you're on. Having met upwards of 500 – 1,000 women online, Twitter is one of my favorite tools to do so. May it be as good to you as it has been to me.

In Chapter 1, we broke down the do's and don'ts of setting up a good profile. Remember that your Twitter photo should be fresh and that your profile is the best depiction of you. Chapter 2 was all about how to search for ladies on Twitter. Unlike MySpace and Facebook, finding women on Twitter presents a unique challenge if you don't know what you're doing. Searching by keyword is your friend so use what's around you in your search efforts.

Chapter 3 broke down every possible type of female you will meet on Twitter. Some of these women should be observed before being contacted. For instance, dealing with the wrong female blogger could seriously tarnish your reputation. Reading and referring to this chapter on a regular basis will help you understand who's out there and how to deal with them.

Chapter 4 revealed how to initiate conversation. This is a problem for most men and reading this alone will put you in a league of your own. Always be original, never brown-nose, and bring a little flair into the conversation. Chapter 5 stressed the importance of sealing the deal and moving the interaction off Twitter. Fellas, always keep the end goal in mind: "Tweet Her *And Meet Her*". There is no reason to exchange tweets with beautiful women and not make any real effort to meet in person.

Chapter 6 called out all of the "Twitfalls" or things that mess up a lot of guys on Twitter. At some point in time I was guilty for all of these things, which lead to a downfall in my game. Pay careful attention to these rules. Chapter 7 shows you how to take your game to the next level. As you become more and more skilled, you should be able to easily pull women off Twitter to an in-person meeting within a day or less. The rules are clear, it's no longer rocket science once you apply the rules!

Chapter 8 was created to address a lot of guys who wanted to get with celebrities. While this may not get you a date with Rihanna, the lessons given in this Chapter have helped me meet a few celebrities and popular Twitter users with a large following. Remember that celebrities do not find "fans" attractive. Be her equal and bring something to the table.

Chapter 9 addressed all of the "high quality" problems you will face once your game reaches new heights. Your main problem will be organizing and remembering all of these women. Using Powerpoint will help you put their faces to their names and prevent potential screw ups. "Coding" keywords in your cell phone will help you do this on the go. And finally, Chapter Ten reinforced some key concepts needed in your pursuits!

Congratulations! You are now ready to *Tweet Her And Meet Her!* When people ask you how your game got so crispy, tell them Flyness coached you! Go get 'em!

glossary of online abbreviations and emoticons

Twitter / Internet Terminology

Tweet – A public status update which is seen by all of your followers and anyone who chooses to view your timeline.

ReTweet (RT) – The art of reposting someone else's tweet, which enables all of your followers to see what they've written.

Timeline – The collection of someone's tweets, in public view on Twitter.

Follow – A feature allowing you to see every public update or "Tweet" someone posts to their timeline

Mention – Any time you make any indirect or direct reference to someone, mentioning them allows them to see your update. A mention is done by including an '@' symbol in front of their user name.

Direct Message (DM) – A feature that allows you to privately message someone. Note: you may only private message someone if they are following you. In order to have a DM exchange, two Twitter users must be following each other.

Trending Topic (TT) – One of the top ten references or words used by Twitter users at any given moment.

List – A way to organize people you follow into categories for easy viewing.

Hashtag – A keyword, denoted with a # symbol. This makes certain terms easier for searching (i.e. "#harlem" or "#ihateunderwear")

Chat Abbreviations

lol – laughing out loud

lmao – laughing my ass off

rotflmao – rolling on the floor, laughing my ass off

smh – shaking my head

ttyl – talk to you later

wtf – what the fuck

str8 – straight

brb – be right back

w/e – whatever

ty ; tx – thank you; thanks

yw – your welcome

j/k – just kidding

For more abbreviations, visit http://www.sharpened.net/glossary/acronyms.php

Emoticons

:) Smiley face; can also use :-)

;) Wink; sly, devious or even polite; can also use ;-)

:(Sad face; can also use :-(

:- Not satisfied; Undecided; not really "feeling it" (one of my favorites)

O:) Angel face ("I'm innocent")

For more emoticon meanings, visit http://www.alphadictionary.com/articles/imglish/emoticons_emot.html

recommended reads

FROM MYSPACE TO MY PLACE: THE MEN'S GUIDE TO SNAGGING WOMEN ONLINE
BY YOUR ROYAL FLYNESS

FROM MYSPACE TO MY PLACE: THE LADIES' GUIDE TO FINDING MR. RIGHT OR MR. RIGHT NOW ONLINE
BY YOUR ROYAL FLYNESS

THE FACEBOOK DATEBOOK FOR MEN
BY YOUR ROYAL FLYNESS

book flyness

Your Royal Flyness has appeared on *Dr. Phil, The Tyra Show, The Planet Abiola Show with Abiola Abrams* (MTV-Made Coach), and has interviewed with syndicated radio shows all across the United States and Canada!

To book Flyness at your school or event, email your request to info@flynesspublishing.com or visit us at www.FlynessPublishing.com for more information!

www.ingramcontent.com/pod-product-compliance
Ingram Content Group UK Ltd.
Pitfield, Milton Keynes, MK11 3LW, UK
UKHW041435180426
11947UKWH00007B/462